EYES OF OPTIMISM AND PUPILS OF FAITH

SHAYAN RAEI

authorHOUSE®

AuthorHouse™ UK
1663 Liberty Drive
Bloomington, IN 47403 USA
www.authorhouse.co.uk
Phone: UK TFN: 0800 0148641 (Toll Free inside the UK)
         UK Local: 02036 956322 (+44 20 3695 6322 from outside the UK)

Published by AuthorHouse 08/31/2021

ISBN: 978-1-6655-8851-5 (sc)
ISBN: 978-1-6655-8850-8 (e)

Print information available on the last page.

This book is printed on acid-free paper.

Contents

About the Author ix
About the book xi

A. Who Am I?

Staring Outside.. 1
Stillness.. 2
As a kid.. 4
Mindful 7
Mission... 10
Promises 13
Collective Lake... 14
Dream 16
Second Nature 17
Thoughts 18
Boots... 20
Train Journeys 22
Life's Yearning 26

B. Where am I going?

True to myself.. 31
Courageous.. 33
Lessons knocking... 34
Keeps you up 35
Choice to choose... 36
Training never stops 38
In touch... 40
Eyes open wide... 43

Clearer view...45
God never said...47
God's arm..48
Garden of my mind..49

C. What is life?

Wonder...53
Yo-Yo..54
Doublethink 57
Allusive 58
Self-reflection..59
The news 61
Nature...62
Ignorance is not bliss.......................................63
Dis-ease...66
Time...68
Spontaneity..70
Personality..74
Worthing...75
Mid November...76

D. Friendships

Very Rare 81
Family you choose..83
Flaky..85
Hold love 86
Wavelength 88
Core 90
Real recognise real 93
Getting deep 94

E. Relationships

When I fall in love 99
Love in mind 102
French girl in Lisbon 103
Test and Games 105
Used to 108
Near miss 110
As of late 112
Still, me then 114

F. Life and Mystery

Mystery in life 119
Wow 122
The secret to living 123
Wizard 129
Onward 132
Technically 134
Family you chose 136
Bring you joy 139
God's projection 140
Architect 142
Kobe Bryant 144
Legends 145
Late October 146
Ruminating 148

G. Three Messages

Love is all 151
Travel alone 152
Reading in-between, the lines 153

About the Author

Shayan Raei is a poet who seeks the extraordinary and the ineffable in humans and the Universe. He possesses a deep curiosity about human life, nature and our spiritual existence. His obsession is fuelled by the peculiarity of the universe and the potentiality of humans, with a strong desire to connect the dots and lift the veil of our reality.

Shayan began his spiritual journey when he was 19. Voyaging on several personal retreats and attending several human development courses across the world during his travels. In the last decade, discovering many unique insights into human consciousness and 'reality'. After contemplation, connecting with his nature and following his souls' journey; as he knows now as the universal language. Shayan has now written his first poetry book, 'Eyes of Optimism & Pupils of Faith.

About the book

This book is a collection of poems that explore what it means to be a human today and a soul, whilst also dancing in-between the mysterious, the wondrous and the beauty in life. Times today are changing at a faster pace, we'd like to attach to what was on other hand, many are now looking towards what is becoming. What is happening around the globe is the growth of human consciousness. This book reflects this shift happening through the poems, anecdotes and Shayan's life lessons, serving towards his evolution.

Human awareness is growing today. Caring about one's contribution is at the forefront of many people's lives today. Many are waking up to their truth. Less are operating as a single entity but part of a larger whole. Our innate knowing of being part of the collective is arising many questions in us today. Tired of feeling disconnected from something sacred within ourselves. Fed up with the news. Tired of conventional ways of living life, the old repetitious order of schooling, earning a living and retirement. Today many are to create a life and want to feel connected to something beyond themselves. Have you ever pondered? What am I here to do? What is my existential nature? Is there more?

Plato once said, 'The unexamined life is not worth living. This poetry book will engage you on a journey through your soul, it will take you into the heights and depths of your mind and the dreams in your heart. Igniting a fire inside of you, connecting you to your soul, stimulating your intrigue and the infinite possibilities you see within your awakening.

Who Am I?

'To be or not to be'
To see or not to see
To free or not to free
To dream or not to dream

Staring Outside

Staring outside
I look higher
I hear - watch this space
A feeling inside me anticipates
Thoughts form...
Exhale on the glass
Draw another portal
As my finger circulates
I look through....
I see in this place
Signs saying
Why wait?

'To be or not to be'
To see or not to see
To free or not to free
To dream or not to dream

Stillness

You can be blind to your own awakening
even if it blinds you at first
you can draw the blinds in
sometimes that's looking at the light more

when you enter the unchartered
there will be light
soon there will glimpses of sight
soon there will be lenses for your eyes
truth and lies, right by your side
truth lies right by your side
truth is not getting it at first
sometimes...

is this guy, in disguise?
look up to this sky and not this guy
with this might and pissed vibe,
with this belief
that he didn't just create the trees
but he's in the trees and grows the leaves,
left her with disbelief

when I also said...

that you are also it, from
the branches to the seed of the tree
heard your name

when the wind blew against the leaves
like you spoke to yourself
as you imagined yourself as the seed
representing to yourself, what you really mean

seeds, reminding us of the new,
growth,
born again
new waves are sure again
bringing new ways for the
sand to formulate again
is that the trend, of no trend?

when does it stop, if the waves
are in constant motion?
how do you stop, this emotion?
look back at this sky, in its vastness
beauty in the emptiness
in it - you see the ocean
reflects your stillness
didn't think of the realness,
you felt what real is

As a kid

My pencils were sharpened on both ends
I was a kid
My pencils were sharpened on both ends

Oddly, I feel like a kid
Even when I'm an adult

I can't be, what I can't be
I can be, what I can be

Just an....
Adult?
A human being?
It's myself
Who I'm being

Phone's taken over TV's
Enough TV, for me
Selective watching
Too many variations of I am not this
This is not me
But not hating on things, just clarity
Of what doesn't matter to me

In the clouds but I planted my feet
Sometimes backward to go forward
So, I use my space more, not so much Insta

Instant
Endless magazine, of your favourite
people in the World
Friends, Family, Celebrities and Idols
Like the best news feed in the World, erhm...

Before it was Televisions taking over radio
Even then, you could still hear them tell a vision
I used to feel anger when I noticed how they
Tell lies, condition and televise a vision
Made me label what's glistening
To avoid consciously crystalling
Then I found out the truth is not out there
It's within
It's within us to define its meaning
The World is beautiful, you feel it
Think, I was always told what to believe in

So.....

Who tells?
Who's listening?
Who turned their back to it?
Subconsciously there, due to their vicinity
Who's persistent with their resistance?
Giving them power, sustaining their reality
What you resist persists, in actuality

Who are those, that just take the
information at face value?

Who takes it in, to a deeper
degree than of face value?
Who takes, themselves as just a
person, as a sole value?

As you watch the waterfall from the
leaf, you follow the rain's drop
Then laugh, because you believed
you knew its sole value
Keep watching
To see something priceless never
had been a sold value
Witness it drop into the ocean
Then, becomes the ocean,
Part of a bigger orchestration

What does your soul value?

Mindful

What of, are you mindful?
No mind is full
Detach
From wherever your mind goes
The gap, you mind for
A no mind is full

First, you hear a lack of awareness
When I say
Pay no mind at all
But you naturally pay attention
Gifted with this awareness
Didn't have to pay at all

There's nothing we really must do at all
'Must'
Words are too narrow
Hear the wider view - inside of you

Gates open then gateways turn
'The observer is the observed'
See what is more, in this segment
Through, Past and Beyond
In the field of the known fragment

If they think they know
Attached to the known

Not ready for what's new and gold
They're stuck on clever
Then be the fool
'A wise person, knows themselves as a.......'
Knows everything will be alright
Everything's cool

Pulling the curtains open
On a dark night of my soul
Waking up the next day, gradually
Seeing what the light's for
Whilst being mindful
Whilst watching the sun rise and the night fall
Feeling lifeful
Seeing what life forms

This love, this connection...
Feels real
It feels actual
Intangible

I am you

You are me

No, I in team....

An I in Mind

I - changed one too many times
So now....
Who's this I that minds?

Trust

There's a you...

In

Us

Mission

Start of December...
Watching space
Stars are contenders
Individually shining bright
Collectively shine brighter

Thoughtful, on a full moon
You're you, for the core you
We all have a duty
Though...duty sounds obligatory

If I have a mission, it is to discover it
To keep playing
To keep uncovering
If I have a mission, a cause
Every day something to look forward towards...
It's crazy I'm here
I must of, in some form been involved
Not the I, in this form
When you look at the World
Each piece has a role to play
A purpose, you would say

What's a mission? A purpose? A cause?
Sounds like we are going to war
A passion?
What if it is to focus on the good every day?

That is a mission
To live in a beautiful state every day
What is it?
A way to be
A desire to achieve?
Do I have the right words, to define its meaning?
Do I have every part of a visual
screening of a mission scheming?
What's a mission really?
It's a feeling, I'm deepening
It's a deep feeling, that wants
to become deepened
Raise up, spread wide, all from inside
If I have a mission, it's a wild horse, I have to tame
If I have a mission, I'm feeling the rain

When the plane is coming down
We put our own oxygen mask first
Before helping others next to us
No instructions - guidance in our favour
If I have a mission, it's to be my own saviour

We all have something
There's something we are called to
Something we are pulled to
Since we are all unique
That's full proof

If I say...If I have mission
It must mean, something
already has my attention

Of what could be a mission
What is driving, the driven?
Similar when thinking a fish is hidden
Causing the water to ripple
Since, you see the momentum
Deep in the waters
You know there is something down there
Never ask, why the water ripples, how it does
So, you'll always say
If a fish is there, it is that making ripples
Yet, a fish exists in water
Birds high in the sky
In this world you find

There is no fish, you are the water,
making all the ripples
There is no mission, you - are the
mission, the question & the answer

Promises

I promise to do this
I promise to do that
I promise everything

Till I begin to notice...
The strings don't tune
The chord goes flat
Till I am out of tune
Till I am out of whack
It's one of days I say and it's just that

It's promises, the ones I create
Even when I feel full and still put lot on my plate
If I throw it on the floor, will it break?
Because I am not ready too
I'm feeling each day more bulletproof
I am maturing with patience and action
Love, kindness and compassion

I've stopped promising this and that
Can't help my wishful thinking
Just things... I want to fall on my lap
I know it'll be there after falling on my back
It's not about falling down
It's up getting up again
I'm promising that

Collective Lake

Schools for creativity
Growing compassion
Deepening empathy
Intuitive-activities
Nourishing energy

Opening spiritually
Because we are more than this
Collectively, energetically,
we're now,
on a level non-physically
here now,
In this time-space reality

Our connection to consciousness streams
We bring ourselves and each-other
Collectively to speed
Everyone benefits
To crystallise the same water
Still as humans
Collectively reap from this stream

We are really the water, in the stream
After all we're more embodying things
Our dreams, our bodies, our thoughts
Sometimes you may lose yourself
Seeing your reflection for long

Seeing yourself in this form
Knowing you are way more

Caught out of the stream for too long
Breathed a new pace to the stream
Till there was no reflection

Laser focus became the whole
Saw the light shine through
Slowed the pace and let go
The stream became a still lake
Found to notice....

Whilst gazing upon, what lied
beneath the surface

As the light shined above, the
depths of your searching.......

Dream

I just had this dream
of me conquering an industry
mastery of self
specifically
thoughts unconsciously in this stream
pacifically
in this dream
I just kissed the
ring on my finger, called myself king
heard a new tone, like a ringer
it was a felling, a signal
felt more like a warm welcome
than a bingo

Second Nature

What comes second nature to you?
Do you have a second for nature? Do you?
You're different, a sacred nature to you
He listens - for the sake of nature
Whispers through you
Hoping you listen

It's not for the sake of it
It's the way of it
In the words of MJ
This is it
In the world of MJ
This is lit

Thoughts

She said, "like, feel and don't think too much"

Told her, "these days I feel too much"

Turns into food for thoughts to munch
"You might say like too much"

And like.... I rather feel and touch

I feel the touch of thoughts come in a rush

That's not from thinking too much

Heard if all you feed is thoughts, you
have nothing to think about

of such

Like walking down the trodden
path, only to walk over it again

building a rut

Now I feed into my senses, walking a bunch

step on a twig, it snapped me back
to the direction I really want

Now I see different avenues and
they all light up at once

Some ideas can fall away, as though
A grain of sand fell into some dust

Still, they do pick up
Like light after dark

What are thoughts?

Similar to clouds in the sky,
that just seem to pass?

Except we can contemplate
Thoughts that we've grasped, to grasp

Let go of some, because
Clouds don't hold weight

Though they look fluffy from afar

Maybe only when it rains

When it comes from the heart

Some see sharp pricks from the rose afar
Some see none from close up

Oh, what are thoughts?

And what thoughts are ours?

Boots

I had the same boots for four years
Didn't wear them out at all
Heard muscles won't grow, if there
is no wear and tear at all

These boots remind me, how
life is so paradoxical
I've changed, the boots with
me - remain the same
I've been worn and torn into a new form
Paradoxically, feel anew and felt older before

People close enough to see your feet, can tell
Can tell if you're getting too big for your boots
Then again, a friend for over ten years,
laughed and said, 'Why you?'
When I once told him, what was true

You can only be you
Instagram is a small reflection of you
So, I hope the next phone, has
higher & wider screens to view
I hope the next Insta update
We can rotate and see wide-captured photos too

How can you really know me, if you
never walked in my boots?
How can I really know you, if i
haven't done the same too?

Train Journeys

She likes coach journeys but
wants to use the train
Thinks about for a sec, but never
will, till she remembers...

No!

Forgot, when she was three,
stood up on the trains seat
Her head by the window near
When her father shouted very clear
"Sit still, don't move! What are you doing?"
Held back natural relief in motion
Eyes kept darted, frozen in commotion
Didn't even shed a tear, lips puckered
Internalized fear, no release of emotion

Not the type of girl thriving off adventure, at all...
Despises the type of girl, who's
dad's let her stand tall
Closes windows shut, on days that are warm
When she got older...
Put down people, not on her 'level'
While they were on their own elevator
It could only be her, to elevate her
The person before her, pressed level one
When they got in, by chance

The doors already closing
She doesn't see an illuminated one,
Pressed one again anyway, in a trance
Pressing buttons in a trance

Back to her story, growing up
Can't picture travelling, she has resistance
Can't imagine fields on fields, in a distance
Can't picture train's on a track, for instance

Grew up, hates men, that do too much
She wants to control her partner,
so he doesn't move too much
Ambition killer, control digger, toxic figure,
See's everyone else as smaller, herself bigger
Doesn't like the silence think
it's void, fills the noise
Doesn't like other's happiness, kills their joy
Remembers back in school, her
crush from the bunch
Who loved to stand on the seat of the bus
She always hated, how she couldn't do the same
She always felt stuck

Now she got older, wants to control everything
That's her rush, wants a partner
who loves to hush
Her last boyfriend told her life is a theme park
She always replied, 'well life doesn't seem fun'
Some day she will go on a ride before she dies

Someday she will
That day she will be alive

One day came when she was older
A man noticed her sat by the
bar and made her blush
She felt a rush and wanted to
stand up and have some fun
Sing like someone who is in love
She got up on the bar and danced so freely
All the men cheered at the
beauty of her femininity
All the men were left in a trance and mesmerised
All the men wanted to dance
with her and be the one

Then suddenly, she jumped
down ran out of the bar
Something made her stop and leave in a rush
Nobody expected it
The man who made her to blush
Thought it was her who decided to have fun
Why did she run?

Guess, he thought, every woman
is supposed to be up
This man didn't know the full story, who she was...
He didn't know she was really hiding
She didn't really know
He poked at it, what she was scared from

She was fearful and it was so real
but, she never knew it was just a scarecrow
It was always there
Once she placed her house in front of it
When we are young, who usually runs home?

All fear leading to hatred
All fear leading to controlling
All fear leading to losing faith in people
Just one internalization, sit down!
Strong energy behind it
Who are you?
You thought, wrong when you
thought it was fine at two!
A dominant thought runs through
What did I do wrong?
As soon as something is done, rings through

Sit still!
You're in danger!!
Stop you're fun, little one!
Sit still!
Where're her toys, the iPad, when
is she going to sleep?
When am I ever going to have my fun?

Life's Yearning

I want to fall in love with my life's journey
Desires burning
Life's yearning

Always pictured the ultimate dream,
a mountain worth climbing
Hardly heard, the mountain is
in me, worth finding
It's worth, to what it's amounting
Something can be true and can exist within me
On my way to the peak of this mountain
To new horizons
Another trip to another mountain
the next morning
This is life's yearning

They want you land to your conclusion early
They all took the flight early
Flying through clouded thoughts
Their flight is not what they thought
Now yearning for a greener lawn
A better thought to teach someone
What they were taught
In a web of the old, they are caught - up

Took a detour to see more
To the pathless for now and for later
You will not find me on the radar

A different place,
A different time the sun is resting
A different outlook in my reflection

Life yearning
Life's mystery
Creates this curiosity

I missed their flight
They all wanted me to take the flight early
I had to fight it, I had to know who was the pilot

Where am I going?

A puzzled look
As I see how this puzzle looks

A lost case
As I stare at this staircase
When did this take place?

Look around me
Most days, in a hurry to find my way

Have I forgotten the grace that came my way?
That will come again

True to myself

A puzzled look
As I see how this puzzle looks
A lost case
As I stare at this staircase
When did this take place?

Look around me
Most days, in a hurry to find my way
Have I forgotten the grace that came my way?
That will come again
See there are open gates
Chose to not believe anyway
If it's just any way

So why try?
Why ask when I ask, why lie?
Eyes wide open but inside frozen
Dark truth or white lies?
White's angelic but dark is telling
So, bring forth to light that which is hidden

Cups' runneth over with potential
Comes running over, pours ten-fold
Have a tray for spillage
My gifts are forbidden
Have a way for spillage

So, I don't verbalise
Tired of my verbal lies

Is it truth, I'm despising?
I just strongly want to be right
Is it my job to be right?

Is being true to myself, my only job in life...

Courageous

I want to be courageous
God gave me these creations
I sought to be courageous
God made me his creation
they say dream dust is contagious
it could take ages

though
wanderlust has you patient
in this playful maze
that you are so amazed with
that you play for and play in
feel that you're made for,
and can be made in

I want an outstanding life
so outrageous,
my idea of a life,
as my favourite
is this life in my favour

Lessons knocking

Again, I learn
Something to know
Again, I think I know

Lessons knock at the door
Introducing themselves again
How are you doing old friend?
I feel you've forgotten me
So, I'm here to remind you again
Perhaps you didn't learn like you thought so
Perhaps you thought - long as you thought so
You've been fighting a lot lately
What else have your thoughts taught?
Ego inflating when justifying again
You're more in the right
Is the only thing these thoughts brought

Lessons knock again
Only to say, next time it's tough love
Either you're too tough or not toughed up
Keep sculpting
You're breaking away, feeling roughed up
Keep your hands on what you're making
Lessons leaves and says one last thing
Breathe

Keeps you up

What keeps you up at night
You got bags under your eyes
You're up excited to death as a child
I see your mind
I see how you want to invite
Me to your mind but I closed doors now
Sorry, but I close doors now
It's my thing
When I say it slowly
Forget it
Sounds like ignorance

I'm the one holding the door
Aiming to peak through too, to see
Though, I'm the master who holds the keys
Then, what is a lock?
If it is not picked, clicked into place
What is a clock?
If it doesn't tock-tick into another place
I clocked, through the time & frame
Synched into the waves
Sink in, another way

Choice to choose

In this life
Your gift is like having tools
You commit
To its avenues
You are the gift

It's your right
To do
Whatever you choose

In your right
It's for you, to allow, not to choose
But chosen for you

You just got a choice to prove
For who?
For you....
Still feel like you got a choice to choose?

Choose to fly......

When you take flight
Don't forget who made you sight
Wings, to spread wide
Sends messages of faith when you fly

On the road of my life's journey
In God's vehicle with my free wheel
You feel thrills?
That's what feels real....

Training never stops

Training never stops
Always learning
The ball is always rolling
If I am not growing
Then I'm dying

Continually becoming aware
Seeing the sun when it's there
Smelling the roses in the air
Whenever you get there

The training never stops
It's always on my clock
If I am growing
Then I'm flying

Continually becoming more
Feeling your heart, at its core
Telling yourself there is more in store
Whenever you get there

Continually being present

That's like walking past a hill
The next day making a reminder
To really look at it when you walk by

Realising the next day, it's huge a mountain
How it made you feel inside

Praised its beauty for raising so high and wide
Took it in, as the clouds faded
whilst they crossed by
Seeing the top clearly and what else that lies

That's similar, to finding yourself, losing yourself
finding yourself, losing yourself
Never losing to create yourself

In touch

She asked, "ever seen a ribbon in the sky?
Ever see a kitten become smitten and sigh?"
I said, "never committed to all of the signs"
Also,
"I'm in touch with my feminine
side, but not all the time"
Though I can't be tight
In the neck to the head like most guys

That some call men
Holding emotion, never cry that's their notion
Stifled energy in just being masculine
When traumatic poison
That one could be masking in
There will be toxic compulsions
Not a robot, release your emotions
Healing
Requires the ocean
Nature's potion
You can't be strong and quick
Whilst ignoring the wind
Ignoring within
Ignorance is not bliss
Set the sails to the wind
Catch the drift?

What if, you just sit...with the wind?
Listen
See how it hits
Your eardrums
Your ears - arms
Giving you goosebumps

Strong - it's forceful
Strong & gentle - it's powerful
Some shake the tree of wisdom
Hoping to get to the root of it
Some, let the wind shake the branches
Dancing with the truth of it
Stepping on gems in a nutshell
In moments of stances

Most of us men are cool and
as chill as the next man
Outrun by thoughts of wanting
to become a better man
Thought's relapse - overlapped
Days we're stuck at flat like we're tired
Feeling torn and uninspired
Indecisive and our actions are divisive
Of course, there is a load on top of this fire
Still, there is a fire

Plus, on this road to gold in which you aspire
You may be told, it's not the
pot or what you acquire

The goal in its entirety
Is where 'you' are required
Live life joyfully, get there
beautifully even if it gets ugly
It may just be the masculine
energy, that's pulling thee
Take time to breathe, if your sails not set
It may be turbulent, at least
you got your 'feet wet'

You can jump ship, but what will that mean?
To the one who flows the sea...
Who wants to see your response-ability
Who sees what you don't yet see...?
With great power, comes great responsibility

Eyes open wide

Fed up and tired
There is only so much you can aspire to
So, what you got to acquire of you
Is draw out what inspires you
The part that requires truth

used to admire destiny
because believed something's
are just meant to be
But what will I even achieve, if
I just sit here - quietly?

Now

Eyes open wide
I'm alive
Hi - not bye
I'm aligned - no idle life
Idealised, in my mind, my ideal time
When I'll deal time
Thought I was a ride or die
Thought I believe that I could fly
I lied, lying down

Saying "not trying now"
Saying "I don't mind'

My eyes were blind,
Knowing the searcher in me
In me - that I will find

Clearer view

Travel through the forest
No specific way to the top of the mountain
To find that clearer view

I chose the raspberry & not the blueberry
Before I had an upgrade for a blackberry
Messages through this journey
Out there and feel there is no signal
You can still capture your story

When you stand at the top of the cliff
It's something to see and nothing to miss
Engaging into the mist of your dreams
Can't see ahead, it seems
The further you go, the more you'll see

Caught the view, in ecstasy
Heard, jump in the sea
Water touches everything
Resembles the infinity

In this early morning
Light shines onto the mist breaking
it, into smithereens
Birds singing happily

The air is cool
Remember last night's echoes from the Wolves
The air improved

Understood, the wolves cry last night
While the camp fire, was burning slowly

Understood why the birds were
chirpy, before Sun rise
Why the fire was kept flamed
through the morning

God never said

God never said,
I'm not guiding you again
God never said
you've let me down
God never said
you have to get it right
God never said
you can't get it wrong
God never said
you are not fulfilling my wishes
God only has love for you

God's arm

God held an arm out, I grabbed on
I held on but looked up again
His arm was gone
So, I thought

I didn't know where I was
It felt like home
I felt whole
Then again, I felt torn
In a way, a good way,
As if I'd teared open a gift

I will hold on
I know how to find him
God's arm's always there
Whenever mine is

Garden of my mind

Standing in front of the garden of my mind
Planting flowers of positive thoughts
I feel the difference, once I've potted
Someone may have implanted
a negative thought
But I never paid attention and they've rotted
My mind will look, to 'find' something negative
So, I maintain my garden whenever I see weeds
Whenever I feel my happiness
Is someone else's responsibility

Daily I stand in front of my garden
Revel in the goodness of what I've planted
Breathing and taking in my own nature
I feel balanced and focused
Standing under a firm tree that's grown
Offering shade, when it's the warmest
Offering shelter, when it's the coldest
Offering nourishment, when I'm hungriest
Nature waters the tree of happiness
With my gratefulness

Wherever I flow
Wherever I fly
Wherever into the unknown, I go
I will stand in front of the garden of my mind

What is life?

Starring into this starry night

The moon's a crescent

Wondering about the Universe

My mood's reflection, in lunar presence

Wondering about my human essence

Tonight, in its luminescence

Wonder

Starring into this starry night
The moon's a crescent
Wondering about the Universe
My mood's reflection, in lunar presence
Wondering about my human essence
In it's luminescence

Wondering...
Pondering...

There mustn't be one route to everything
There must be one root to everything

Looking to the moon
Asking for the truths and blessings
Renew the message
Earth is always the new heaven
Writing in a few sentences
I want God's presence
Reading in between the lines
To get his message and true essence

Yo-Yo

The World stops still, for a minute.
While the World - still till infinite...
Though, never still, is it?
Sparkling

The motion of duality vs the notion of Yolo
The World stops and spins at once, like a Yo-Yo
The calmness amongst calamity
How to speak of the unknown?
Can only see as one goes
The solitude and solidarity
Praying for the World's restoration
Our own rejuvenation requiring separation
In times like these, we pay for our attention

How does a bird fly without falling first?
How's does a rainbow shine
without the storm before?
How does hunger come without
the thirst before?

The World is still for some spring cleaning
The World is still for all to bring meaning
The World is spun for perceiving
The World is spun for no ceiling

His show must go on
I love a show, when I know all it's lines
This must be it - doesn't look like it now
Then so be it
Tremendous faith in everything I'm not seeing
Have a sense of my soul and why I'm breathing
Knowing my true self, is always believing in it all
We are doing the best we can
We are taking what we got, can't fault us
Not always seeing how it all happens for us

Now there is locusts
God sent a swarm of infectious insects like flees
To attack like bees to free the streets
In Africa, locus of the disease from the East
Now COVID-19, everyone must flee the streets
From the West, Europe and to the Middle East
All must be at their nest and at ease
Remembering this life for its beauty and fragility

Infinite times a vase is given
Forever a vase is loved and forgiven
Too many times vases never mend when broken
Too many ways a vase is not meant to get broken
Sometimes vases have no water for flowers
Sometimes we take this life for granted
Forgetting it was already a gift
From when it all started
If you're broken
Glue with gold between the cracks

Is that scar or scratch?
Things reminding I'm human
Is that your hand?
Some say it's mapped
Give me the palm of your hand
Now tell me what is his plan?

Maybe something is on the way,
now it's andale, andale
It was under-layed, now it's under-way
Maybe, because Gods timing is never on delay

Doublethink

because of the apparent evil
there are people as paralegals
figuring out what powers legal?
the power leagues of parrots lethal
would know systems
even those that are see-through
don't empower people
that make them feel like empowered eagles

well...
If designed for caring people
stuck in the cage of what's fair and equal
never flown above for a different view
never flown away from the one's that feed you
though, neither did they

from their parrots keepers
as their parent's repeaters

carrot and stick teachers
made apparent preachers

quick info lechers
strict into teachers

keepers of finders
never daring seekers

Allusive

Illusion and Lucid sound too alike

To assume in a black and white
Illusion and stupid rhyme

When I seek the right meaning for life

Allusive lines defining life
Elusive to define

Illusive and lucid rhyme

When I seek the right screening for life

Self-reflection

How do you even define life?
Or yourself?
We are ineffable
Too expansive to be descriptive
Words can't dissect us into something definitive
Though...I was told, feel the
words closest to home...

Alan Watts once said, trying to define yourself
Is like a knife trying to cut itself
Is like teeth trying to bite itself
Waiting for a stream of thoughts,
to define yourself?
I look down at the water
I'm watching myself reflection
I am

I look down at the water
the currents not in my favour
I want a new flavour in what I want reflecting
I put my energy into motion
I altered my e-motion
The currents started changing
I guess it's the frequency of the water
I guess it's my vibration

The changes in the outer world around us
The inner change of the world within us

Causing this deep self-reflection
On a higher level we all want to be vibrating

Why do we speak of energy so much?
What time are we in and what are we making?
I don't see Shayan in the water,
when I look deeper
I see the ideas, possibilities that peep up
I may not see anything, when I close my eyes

If life is a play...
Stories have extreme power
Channelling us to a new program
Programming us to a new channel

There's a new story to our journey
We see today, more are sensing oneness
A real sense of communal self-reflection
A change in the air, a scent of consensus

Where do we like to be heading?
School's still reciting Henry's be-headings
History in some form repeats itself
Depending on the headings
Yet, I see a new beginning

As mankind, we ask when are we ready?
Because some are in control, telling us
We are not ready

The news

What do we have to say for today?
What does the news say, as of late?
I guess I'll just read that page
Click on it tomorrow again
I guess that's where I'll get my rage
Don't worry, it doesn't affect me
It's something I'm used to
I don't like to admit it
The news I consume is my fuel
I'm sorry it's taken a dump on my personality
Since it affects my personal reality
I'm in a defensive shell
If everything was destined not for money
Then I guess we'll see more good
If everyone was just kissing and hugging
Then I guess you'll see me in a good mood

Whenever we turn on the news
Fear sells, he sells and she sells
Seashells by the seashore
I hope you'll finally take that trip
Just to reflect by the sea more and see more

Nature

Nature said,

"book shop there,
Knowledge is power,
look inside an hour,
Don't forget your power"

Before I left...it whispered

"Just accumulating knowledge is ignorance
Now don't be sour,
Knowledge of self is power!"

Information can be like the past - dead
In respect - useless
When attaining knowledge of
which you're unaware
I heard real learning is unlearning
to become aware
Then to learn from there

Ignorance is not bliss

Heard the quote, 'Ignorance is
bliss' it was always there
Parrots are still beautiful, though
they repeat what they're told
So, I guess we got to stay ignorant to the end
I think that quote exists, only to
something it should be ignorant with
Encouraging ignorance as a state
of 'nirvana' towards bliss?
Really that type of bliss is self-
defeating conformity
With respect to a reality
That one didn't consciously create
By default, we engage
This decision is unconsciously made
Who has the power, where is it placed?
Inside

Ignorance is bliss, hmm
I don't hear this, to stay oblivious,
because ignorance is...
A nap, a way to sleep of who we are, you
can be awake and still be asleep....

Why throw the word bliss around like that....
Poor wording, no wordsmith

Word spins got the world spun
No fun

Is it bliss?
Attached to accumulated knowledge of self
Attached to detaching from it all
Instead of engaging in life dearly
Breaking away from what we accumulated...
Seeing ourselves clearly

Beyond matter, is beyond what matters
Since thought shapes things and
energy moves matter
I'm manifesting my inner-world for the better
Seeing what exists inside but
not becoming ignorant
To the destruction from the corruption
Though not ignorant to seeing what is in me
If I am ignorant
I may be ignorant to the enormous power in me
It must be to infinity

As we evoke, we evolve
We don't know anything
Till magic shows us, what we know

So!
Bliss from all knowledge of what
works in this world of matter
Not a state of oblivion

Not ignorance
Since....
Knowledge of self is power
Still, what is bliss and how are we relating to it?
They tell us in the World what matters
Happiness is the answer!
Ignorant ends to that answer
Like a drunk driver, with no head lights to nirvana
Bliss looks the sky and happy
sounds like the weather

How about I get connected every day?
So that breeze never leaves

Knowledge is power, for an hour
Knowledge of self is power, for eternity
That's higher power, that's our higher self
Any book on it, you'll find them on a higher shelf

A librarian noticed, when there
would be books on the floor
Some knew the light was there,
knew they'd never will face the light,
if they'd think it's too bright
still placed it back on the top shelf
when they picked it up
that decision was innately theirs

Dis-ease

Dis-ease causes disease

This ease causes release

Release opens me to receive

More thoughts of ease to retrieve

Then conceive of things more fulfilling
Such as healing

I can't write a list and just sum up
Everything I am grateful for
Then be all happy and just jump up
I've must take a few minutes
To breathe, to release and to put myself in ease
Then I'm ready to raise my vibe, it's my therapy
Very therapeutic, I can find
anything to appreciate
Whenever I'm happy or I decide to
bring myself to this moment
Then hold it, bring another pleasant
thought and build on it
It's spiral staircase upward
Negativity can't spiral when I do this
I build a shield from it
More so, I feel fuel from it

Nowadays science demystifies
The mystical to make it literal
We can produce our own healing chemicals
Many cases of healing everyday
Many miracles

Electric thoughts sending waves
Magnetic heart attracting waves
Electric- magnetic waves
When I lay my hand on my heart
Breathe in and feel ease
Mind and heart in sync
To my natural well-being, I'm connected
Its beyond me to know I'm always protected

Time

Can never tell the back of your hand
Only when you turn back in time

You know, what you're cooking up
Still, don't know its taste
Only when you look into the ingredients
To see what you like to include, in what you make

Couldn't tell the back of my hand
or even who I am...
Didn't ask of this self-reflection this much...
A period, I didn't connect anything
Witnessed connections happen naturally
Collect these thoughts
Look back, to connect these dots

Hands on the clock
Designed as a straight line
At its end, an arrow points at the time
But in life, there is ups, there's declines
Twists and swirls, in this world
Life's is not so linear to just point and define
Life is mysterious, so we point and define
Everything is relative
A period can drag or can fly
early feels late
When you don't appreciate

There really is no-thing, such as time
Created, to know, when the day's turning to night
Before it was gauged, from
melted candles, in sight
What is time?
If we're always here and never died
What is time?
If we don't live, while we are alive

Timing has a way
and
There is a way, with time

Spontaneity

You say you're somebody for
Spontaneity, from the moment
Because you'll
Spawn to eighty in a moment
You're always preaching
Live your life
Own it
But I realised after that moment

You intercept information
Hardly inspect it, in introspection
I'm asking questions,
To remind us of that time,
Which faded, like a smoke ring
Want to wake you up
Because you sleep-talk on woke things

A synchronicity showed up twice
twice like a deja vu thrice
You chose not to believe in it
We were showed concrete evidence
of divine intervention
You turned away
Asking for something concrete
It's evident
You didn't want to soak in its meaning

That's when I realised
Your mind is your real eyes

So true
That's why you couldn't believe
what you're seeing
When it showed you
Probably, why you wrote perspective as a caption
For a pic, of yourself, overlooking a view
Not realising the view
And perspective is really inside you
Maybe the view made you
sense a new perspective
Though, the environment is in you

Does the path, change your view?
Or does your view, change the path
leading you to a different view?

Seek what's the truth
'Truth is pathless' - Jiddu

An open mind
Opens lines for communication
For interpretation
You follow a religion
So, why are you afraid?
Say you know God
Why the tension?

We all have angles
Like a top Google definition

What you see is what you make it
And what read into, is what you're making
What are you making of this?

All I was saying in our conversation
There can be more to
One's operation
Then that came into our eyes
In 'time', proving to me
You're blind
To your ignorance
For your ego's salvation

Always speak like you know
what's right for my life
Never listening to life
Never witnessing life
Never tuning into the serendipity of life
All you talk about is - live your life

To you means - another flight
That's part of it
Believe, you're so whole now
But always point at other people's holes
Life's a mirror
It's true

When you see the lack in them
You're seeing the lack in you

Conceptualise God
While I ask for an open dialogue

Why...
Speak high of opportunities
Then
Speak down on possibilities
What for?

Can only point at others being
too hot or too cold
Since you're just lukewarm

Personality

Stranger than fiction in my life
Has become my diction no lie
I prayed for creativity
When feeling friction creatively
Listened with my eyes
Finding what hidden means
In my personality
I stayed where it's heavenly...
Stayed in my curiosity...
Towards my personal reality

Doing life's thinking under stress
It's like painting with one brush so rushed
The object is used so quickly to its bitter end
How can you be objective and bitter in the end?
Does it make sense?
It's like wanting to make peace
when you want revenge
It's like wanting to be free but
value security till death

I want to be running free
Asking myself what even is security?
A life of uncertainty is met certainly
Not all those who wander are lost
A life on my terms is met with certainty

Worthing

I arrived at Worthing to a meditation
retreat, on a Friday evening
Hoping by the end I have
found a better meaning

To this gift called life
To my own dance, I'm leading
I will continue
Without fully knowing which way I'm heading
For all the beauty the Universe has to uncover
I will meditate
So, a clear mind can discover

That I am an energy
Flowing just like a river
Breaking all mental barriers
So, I can enter wherever

Another dimension is what I might see
I'll practice longer so it's not only a peek
A day where I am and the
superior intelligence meet
Is where I will also rest and gleam

Mid November

Mid-November...
Looking at a picture of me at school...
I never was a deep thinker
This pose, begs to differ
Rich from life
I sometimes beg to differ

I need time with this all
I don't want to be another parrot
Look colourful but still a parrot
Saying things like....
I feel time has no form

Always interested in the truth
Whether it be...
What the weather means...
Could mean anything on any day, to me
Reality is what you choose to feel
Create what you feel
Always been interested in the truth
Whether it be what they're telling me...
Some people like to paint a vibe
Ruling white
Behind a looming sky
A light touch with a white brush
For a ray of light

Whoever chooses measures
Can be rulers, as far as it goes
Not a question of skin tone
I don't want to travel every
centimetre of this rabbit hole
We know there is a World, from
which we felt we built
I love our beautiful cities, rich
with culture & history
Though what we feel inside is real
We manifest what we feel, then make it real
Energy carries a field, from which they yield
Higher energy, the new world, is being built!

I am not thinking on this topic solely
I listen, as my heart speaks
Thank my heart
As the past talks, whilst the present speaks
I watch, as my soul leads

It's not this end of endless information,
To its end, I am chasing
It's the end, of this pen
To its endless end, I am creating

Friendships

People change like seasons - even you

At the core, still you, at the root

Just different seasons, call for a different you

Very Rare

Not a pessimist
Optimystic
Though...
Very rare to find a genuine friendship
That lasted from eight
Till they were eighty-eighty
Didn't you know?
Not so bad, when you know
These things end, for the greater good for you
Thus the greater good of all

The way nature be
People want to grow like trees
Naturally
Then maintain their seed

People change like seasons - even you
At the core, still you, at the root
Just different seasons, call for a different you
Naturally when the seasons come
Like the leaves, people will leave too
Sometimes they can fall off, when you branch off
That's natural too

Something called, being with the flow
Realising, you can't do this on your own
Accepting that you don't know

Whilst the other, always feels to be in 'control'
Of you, of life and feel's over-thrown
Not yielding to what nature, undergoes
The flowers bend to the wind, to not get blown
Learning to let go

Conditionally, told to see life's inner-
quest as life's inner-battle
That's why we divide, pick sides and start wars
What side is real?
What's sidereal? Are all stars born?
Listen to the force - Star Wars
Messages are passports
I got to catch that film, Sidereel or Netflix?
God's online, we all need our net fix

Family you choose

They say your family is whom you choose
They are your friends, the struggles
Together, times you've been through
The ones you allow to know you
Through and through
Friends are family whom you relay your truth
I left one or two WhatsApp groups
Because I felt distant, from whom I knew
Hardly picked up the phone, to ask what's new?
Social media, makes me feel I
know you, but just a version
I miss your stories, in person

I forgot how it felt to miss you brother
I forgot how it felt to miss you sister
I forgot how it felt to miss you

Maybe it's just life and it's meant to be
Maybe we give priority to this maybe mentality
But I guess sometimes, it is meant to be...

Sometimes you forget the affect
you have on your friends
You forget how it all began
Good friendships can be the
sweetest thing on this land

Friends become family
Connected to a point unconditionally
I don't want too many rules and conditions in me
Times I remind myself to let
things go unconditionally

For the love I want to give
For the love I want to receive
For the way I want to live

Not every friendship is smooth
You want as friends to communicate on any issue
It strengthens you
It allows you to know yourself better
Makes, you love your friend more
Who wants to know themselves too
Friends are a reflection of you

What is friendship?
If we don't support each-other with
the same love families do?

Flaky

Do you feel a void when you're avoided?

Can't define why some people pretend
Pump you up, like a steroid hit
Then, they make you feel avoided
When they avoid it

Can't avoid questioning their choices
More so, when they lack knowledge
To acknowledge this avoidance

Flaky snow usually doesn't sit well
Has little substance
Can't stick around like foil
Something, one really can't roll with

Hold love

Learned the significance of friends
Who have boundaries and keep empathy
Pray to never fall into petty-thinking
Whilst making myself a priority

We've all had people meeting needs
As a consequence losing values
Losing values fulfilling selfish-needs
Compromising the means by its ends
By any means rhymes with enemies
Some people can't speak truthfully
We just have to accept we are
like that to a degree

Yet some can be too misleading
Penetrate those who are really caring for them
They can have a lasting effect
Except, only in reps
Similar to a friend, for a while strangely pretends
Each time they act petty, they lose your respect

No poem, can depict what I'm really trying to say
I can't force it...
Similar to slow drips from the faucet
Some people will take what you got to give
Till it's dead, no water left

My heart is the faucet
Pouring into a sink bowl
Depth with boundaries holds love
As I study its mould

Wavelength

Daily....
Speak your own waves
Then as you proceed to seek your own way
When the tides get high
You will see, who's really on your wavelength
Seek those, open to learning
the value of uncertainty
Not those too sure
Forever and ever waiting for the wave's rest
Fighting with you and fighting the wind
Not having their sails set
Small regard for self-love and silently needy
Pridefully
Make you feel guilty for not
catering to their feelings
Asking where the tray went

Sometimes being selfish means no
I can't engage in that
News or politics, same difference
Selfish enough, for zero desire in complaining
I can't come plain
It doesn't fuel me; can they gauge in that?

Defeatist conversations, stirred
in a negative blend
With the same friends, has lost its flavour

Now I pretend I don't know
where the tray is, to cater
Now I'm adding missing ingredients
To make something great
To savour

When I get to cooking
I'll have something to offer
More than just a pinch of solitude
I need a hint, of a solid truth
Sprinkle on the top, zest for life
My aura is a beautiful aroma
That is coming through

Life tells me,
if you want all your dreams to happen now
It's like getting all the food,
you want to eat for the rest of your life, right now
Don't worry about how the rest will be
For now, play with some recipes

Core

I talk about my tree,
You see my roots, deeply
Pointed to a tree you love and grew
The next day,
You thought I wouldn't remember the route
The height of your tree or the colour of your fruits
The next day,
You took me to a tree, you barely knew
The one you take everybody too
Told me about its problems and its joys
I empathised and cherished it too

Though, you really never shared your fruits
From the day I noticed you to
Maybe that time was a fluke
One day, we were together
You pointed again to the other tree
Which was not yours
I see an artificial root
I see an artificial you

Many people interfered with your tree
Picked some fruits
Made you forget nature
With no intention to
Made you forget, the way
That trusting is in you

The next week
You have people dancing to your tree
I see this tree doesn't exist too
Though some give you attention for this tree
I can only give you attention to the part of you
I know or knew - the part which is you
I can only give you me,
To the degree, I am me
Sorry if I am too real
I am not sorry that I am me
If that makes me real

The day you showed me another tree
That didn't belong to you
It hurt me inside
I see you keeping a super-official vibe
The more you feed me lies
I feel a superficial vibe

The next month
More are dancing to your tree
Not your real tree
These days, you keep for you
Can't help to think, what did people do to you
For you not to really share your fruits
Someone I know having such deep roots
I wanted to be a someone
Whom openly trusts
Presents my fruits to you
Showing what trusting can do

You keep a lid on it
So, you come sealed
Similar to dried fruit
Though the package is clear
I can see right through

You want to show you
Share your tree

The real you

I know there is more
To the core

Real recognise real

you're not a friend,
you care are about you,
in the end,
maybe you're so weak,
you don't realise when,
you should return the favour again,
so, I keep on helping you,
my hand I lend,
and pull you
from your depths,
in my giving nature,
I don't just lend,
I give and give
my own energy I expend
at your expense

what about myself?
when bad times come around,
If I'm down,
you never hear a sound,
that's why you're deaf
with your heart, you don't listen
I've witnessed

where is your empathetic nature?
be the type of friend that I am
real recognise real
you'll never recognise who I am

Getting deep

Never understood it, whenever I
heard, 'we're getting deep'
In my life, on 4 or 5, different
occasions, I've heard it
Usually, one would say it from a
bunch who were listening
On different occasions, I was talking or listening
Each time, the person said it,
Excited and looking perplexed for a minute
As if the depth of their thoughts became vivid
Seeing something beneath the surface
Sparking their curiosity
It was the spell, that unlocked their arm-bands off
Entertained by the shallow-end long enough
Tired of knowing exactly where
they stand, standing up
Now, no position and swimming deeper
Floating and legs are like they're dangling
Those conversations, full of emotion
Roller-coasting is when your legs are dangling

A raft wasn't chosen,
No intention to stay on the surface
Where they're sure
Conversations flowing more in ands & ors
No oars and in a natural tide

Drifting somewhere out of sight
but far from losing sight
To find with no expectation is
a surprise – even better
To flow there, to go deep, to go there, together

Conversations, where there's
connecting, projecting,
questioning, expressing

Full of mystery and delight
Is when you paraglide
Legs like they're dangling in the sky

Relationships

Two meet

Nothing to complete

A destiny

Two destined to be

Will feel like a bonus

The gift within the gift

The lift within the lift

When I fall in love

When I fall in love, I see beautiful faces
When I fall in love, I land in beautiful places

Finding love is a mystery
Is it to love, we are toasting?

A relationship gives you perspective
How do you know what you want,
If you don't know, what you don't want
Have you ever been in one?
With who, are you comparing her to?
You're comparing you
Realising who you are
Realising who you are with her too

God's greatest creation is women
They bring out different sides to you
Don't be confused, when she opens through
Realise, there is another side to you
Now figuring, if there is more
It can never be the girl
You settle on yourself
When you settle down to just do
Sometimes you get her
Still feel there was something else in it for you
Think of the person you want to be
In the longer view, time for you

You may need to move to space
If she's a keeper
She'll give you space to move

Can never walk around with an empty cup
Expecting to be filled up
If I believe, she completes me
She can deplete me
Since I expect her to fill me up
She might expect the same
It can put us in a funny frame
This is not how I picture love

I want to know true love

You complete me, by cheersing me with your cup
I'm in love with how you love yourself
It brings out yourself
Beautiful - funny as hell

I fill my own
You fill your own cup
Your appreciative of your life
Grateful for living your own story line

Whenever - I do marry
I want it to a celebration
It's a celebration of our continuation
The cherry on top
Is the continuation of celebrations

Two meet
Nothing to complete
A destiny
Two destined to be
Will feel like a bonus
The gift within the gift
The lift within the lift

A bonus, is unexpected
I know, life to be this way
I know, I'll meet my wife this way

Adventurous way to it
Unexpected relationship
Since no-thing will be our expectation
The thing is, our love, our appreciation...

Love in mind

There is no such thing as time
So, when I see you, it's always love at first sight
We rise in love, right? Not fall...
Though I find myself then
Falling in love with you
over & over again

Every time
Every single time...
If I have the words
I'd say it's your eyes
When I look into them
Words can't describe
How I feel inside
When you come to mind
I can't hold back my smile
How much, I see you and me
side by side,
How much I, want you as mine
How much longer, till I say I...

French girl in Lisbon

Life is random
Don't know what to expect
Excited to accept what's next
When I look through finer lens
I say less and do more
For who for?
For me of course
Then I happened to meet you
Am I off course?
Universe says, 'Things happen, to meet you'

But I do not fall in love so easily
Though when I was with you
I feel for you, naturally
No guard, gradually
You played games
I played too
Realising
Me and you are the same
Yet so unique in our own ways

That's why you were attracted to me
Like the paint your draw with
Felt appreciative of me like
The page you draw in

That's why I felt attracted to you
Like the lines I write in
Felt appreciative of you like
The meaning I rhyme with

I knew
Your beautiful eyes
Spelt wonder in you
Before I wandered with you
Now... I wonder about you

You know
Life's for living for the moment
Just being open
You know life has no problems
Yet, transcending challenges for owning
So, why do I feel there's something
for me, you are solving?

Test and Games

I'm finding myself daily
You have tests and these games for me
Hoping I found you
I don't think you have tested your games
These days, I can't be me around you

Your overzealously ways
Creating jealousy games
A sort of attention you aim to maintain
Till the point the games are not cool
You are moving into disrespectful ways
Making me feel no way about you
Forget a girlfriend
Something a girl who's a friend, shouldn't do

Perhaps I should've been the bad boy this time
Do you want a man or boy in your life?
I know a girl like you...to a girl like you
Good boys don't know two from too....

Lately, you want define your own trust
Maybe to you, feel you've trusted too much
Trying to hold me down, hold up
Maybe you're not patient for love
Lately, you feel a type of way
Awfully strange with your games

Made me type away
Maybe, you should give it a break

when uncomfortable feelings get mixed
there will be a twist
you definitely gave it a twist
maybe you should call it quits
to save a friendship
because
not enthused with your games
not so concerned about your whereabouts
then don't expect me to answer,
whenever I'm out

so quickly with me, you put your guard down
I was so appreciative
so quick, for you to judge that right now
with questions, trying find what's what
right now

you delayed my sense of commitment
when you act like to something
I should be committed
when in the moment, with me,
you can't just live it
see where it goes, see where it is heading
expectations of me, what are you expecting?
turning your games into disrespecting
as if I was with you, now you feel neglected

as if I promised you my love,
now you feel rejected
you act so strong, though you want protection

that's deep stuff
you want to be easily pleased
but you don't just want a pleaser
that's deeper

it's a journey to your heart
to love
when the time comes
you will meet the one

Used to

I know my heads moved on
but I'm physically still tied to you
my hearts moved on
yet I'm still energetically tied to you

our love - its depth
the amount of love - was there,
breathing neck to neck
your head laid on my chest
used to stroke your hair
whilst you expressed how you felt
trying to move on
but my emotions still in debt
think one day, I am over this feeling
then the next day
I think of you
right now, not having you
Is not what I'm used to

Growing and breaking down
Becoming anew
I put it in a nutshell
Then cracked the middle
To let the light through
Feels like I'm allowing to

feel what I feel now
No more fighting through

No time limit on it now
Till I become myself again
Till I get used to - this new

Near miss

Hear this what I fear is
You think leaving him
Is never a near miss
It's like escaping a building
That's tearing now
You know where the exits are
Still at the top staring down

He's not your lover - your white knight
He's your joker on your darkest night
Came searching for you
Knows where you are
Sees windows blazing out fire
This is time he will save you
You see it in his eyes
Then you notice he doesn't have it inside
Or want it...

Hesitates...
The same eyes, once looked into you
Used to penetrate
It's as if it was all a lie
What was made?

Never a became man
Because there is a journey for that
Never made for you
Because there is a story to that

Plus, why can't you be your own saviour?
The one is waiting for your trust
Waiting for your self-love
To love yourself enough
Otherwise, he's just a crutch
Someone to use, not cherish but to clutch
Someone you lose their essence when you touch
It's all from a place of control - rush
You lose touch
I know because once I did
With the one I was with

'No, no don't touch me right the now'
Why did he go away?
These silly games should be left
In my teenage days,' your heart says
Your mind keeps repeating these games
You're not giving up
When deciding to give it all up
It's always been given a break...
Till your heart aches...
You're not opening your heart
When you go back for another heart break
When is enough – enough?

I know this time something will give
Because how much more can you take?
Till you take more hits to your face?
When will you see?
That it shouldn't have never been hate

As of late

We'll just part ways
What will give...
What will this part take?
Feel something for you
Something we've part-taken
My heart
You can have it
Without it...
I feel a heart-breaking
If I know somethings not right with you
My heart's aching

Care enough about you
Feel your joy and your pain
Why don't you want me to go?
You make my heart stay...

Too much of you
May not be good for me
You're part cake
Multi-layered girl
Sweeter as I strip parts away
My luck
Want to call you my love
But can't rush to play the part
To just have a part to play
How'll this part play?

As of late
Have a spot in my hearts place
Writing my book, found us on the same page
Gave me a look, now I'm thinking
I want to be true to you in all ways

There for me
There for you
Heard my heart say
Liberating music, as I pictured you
Heard my heart play

Still, me then

Love is something I try not to manage
Since if I do, I may not have it
I got my guard up but talking with you
I understand it

When I think of your baggage
I think of travel and no damage
Tell me the truth always
Taking things out
You're messing up the fabric
Saying it's too heavy
Though, we can't fly without it
Layers to you like a cabbage
Is it the dark and ugly, you think I can't fathom?

If I ask, I want to know how God planned it
Beautiful - he painted you on his canvas
In this life of yours, it is tragic and magic
You're sweet and a savage
It takes forever for me to fall
In the meantime, I'm candid
Leave an air of mystery because
I don't know yet there is a you and me
But like the alphabet
A - let's be then see
I got to be your best friend first
It makes sense

Lying I can't tolerate
We get what we tolerate
You've already opened up so much
When I'm getting to know you
I won't rush, that's just how I operate

I live in depth and under the sea it vibrates

Why wait?
Why don't we just fly away....
For time's sake
We can't
For lying sake

I can't give you me when you
don't give yourself truly
I like a girl who is clever for the better
Once you have me, you got me forever
I thought you knew me like an old soul
We were just getting things on a roll
Maybe you didn't even know...
The way I speak, it's always the
same enthusiastic tone
Whatever happened...I've gone cold
And I don't even think you'll know
I just don't have too many questions anymore
It's a cabbage that rotted whilst
I kept peeling for more

Maybe it's the wrong season
Maybe just wanting you is freeing
Maybe it's ourselves we're deceiving
Maybe I just to need to learn
It's still me then....
Till it be me and another being
In love and in freedom

Life and Mystery

I know, where your innocence lies
Inside...
Your purity
Your love
Your belonging...
Divine

Mystery in life

I see the misery in life
I see the mystery in life

I see both, at the same time
Sort of like, when I look into your eyes
I feel I see you here
Your soul at the same time
Your mind might
Though, your eyes, never lie
I know, where your innocence lies
Inside...
Your purity
Your love
Your belonging...
Divine

I feel the misery in life
I feel the mystery in life

Disintegrated lands more natural
Then plans of, disintegrating man
Walk the talk, who's talk?
Many are coming to their true selves
Many are lost without any spiritual guidance
Goals and insights from mentors
To-do lists with reminders

For a second, I had to discharge
Also, means from another
person's mental discharge

So, no books in my backpack
For now
Perhaps just one, that speaks to me
Some food with a drink
As I go off to nature which teaches me
To have a think

Stimulating my intrigue
With me
With the world
Within me

What if...
If I just sit here, with the water
If I just sit here, with the sky
If I just sit here, with this tree
If it just sit right here...
What if...

There's always been man's search for meaning
Opening the heart continually for its freedom
Coming in touch with his being,
not always lost in chasing
Meaning in achievement, without the meaning

Becoming great feelers in what
they're are fulfilling
There have always been these human feelings
There's always been a mystery, a
way to one's revealing's...

Wow

I look to God at all times with both eyes
Not just through the hard times
I see her in everything
You see in everything, is where Christ is
and that's how you find him

Seen why you never cry sis, in a crisis
it's not cold in your heart
like someone from Isis
or another person filled with hate
not trying to discriminate
that just had its place
like perfect timing

they say for even for those in your life
forgiveness is where the ice is
to always be for giving
not just for getting
to be present,
for the gift of life's prizes

The secret to living

I was in Noordwijk for a course
I still remember that trip
If I could, I would relive it
I remember it so vivid
Learned a quote on the course
By Tony Robbins
'The secret to living is giving'

On my last night in Noordwijk
There was an annual firework show
Right by the shore
Opposite the hotel, right by the course
Looked so beautiful to me
Watching fireworks explode in
jubilation above the sea
The sky sparkled for a moment in time
The sea shimmered, as the sky
flashed and shined

Me and others from the event
Celebrating life
Danced our last night away in
the club and just before
We had our own party on Netherlands's shore

The next day I awoke to a bright morning
Packed my bags and said
"Amsterdam I am on my way"
Before, I passed the corridor,
from the cleaner's way
I gave her five euros, as a token of gratitude
For cleaning my hotel room, during my stay

Left my hotel, I walked down
the street to catch a bus
As it arrived, I hopped on and
realised – there was Lisa
A friend I made on the course, she
was leaving at the same time
We talked about our experience at the course
The time we partnered up, for an
exercise involving a dance
How much we were both into
it, how we got intimate
We shared stories that were unforgettable
Personal moments that were meaningful
Now sharing the same route
to Amsterdam central

Laughed all the way to the local train station
To catch our train to Amsterdam central
It's as if everything was going to plan
Both going with the flow
We made it on our train
Put our bags down and took a seat

As the train began to leave
We continued our conversations, joyfully

Suddenly, a ticket officer came
by, looking very stern
Asked me first, "tickets, tickets"
Then he took Lisa's as well, without saying a word
And passed mine back and took
a double look at hers
He said, 'you must pay a 50 euro
fine, this ticket is invalid'
I saw the look on Lisa's face, she couldn't concur
Shocked to take an unexpected
cost from what'd occurred
Especially in such a lovely time and moment
Whilst feeling life was jovial,
the way life was going
It was silent for a moment, our
conversations were not flowing
I asked her if her ticket is the right one
It seemed she had to pay a 50 euro fine
Then the ticket officer - out of no where
Said, in very nice way
'Take this young man for a 50 euros
dinner, then you don't need to pay'
I couldn't believe it, I started laughing
Lisa laughed too; her eyes gleamed with relief
It wasn't the money, but the situation
that suddenly nearly came to be

The ticket officer, smiled at her
and gave me a wink
As if to say, I got you guys and now I'll leave

I continued laughing, I just couldn't believe
Whilst my head fell to my knees
As I picked my head up
See 5 euros held in front me
"I want you to have it, it's yours"
Lisa was pleading for me to take her money
Very unexpectedly
I replied, "I appreciate this Lisa,
that man actually let you off"
Lisa, in joy and gratitude
Just said, "It's yours"

All of a sudden, I found a meaning
I remembered the morning
As I was leaving
Giving 5 euros to the lady who was cleaning
Lisa said, "it's meant to be"
Her eyes staying wide open & glaring
She added, with a sense of enchantment
"I trust this feeling"

Our train had finally reached
Amsterdam Central station

Now we were ready to part ways
See what else life has planned

She was heading back to England
I was heading to Rotterdam from Amsterdam

Before saying our goodbyes
We rejoiced how great it was
meeting on this course
Even more funny and double as interesting
How we stumbled into each
other on our way home
How out of everyone we both met
We both connected with each other the most

After speaking for a few extra minutes
Lisa's train to the airport was soon to arrive
We started becoming sentimental
Both chuckled about Amsterdam
How it's beautiful and mental
Before embracing each other one last time
We shared a kiss good-bye
Then I wished her a safe flight
She did as well, for whenever mine arrived
We were departing from a very experiential time
We weren't a couple saying our good-byes
But a lady walked by and embraced it
As if we were the type
She loved the sight of lovers in her sight
Lisa and I, keep in touch from time to time
Reflecting our love and gratitude for this life

I went on exploring Amsterdam
Before my trip to Rotterdam
After a few hours passed by
I got hungry and went to buy food
Whilst waiting in the queue
A lady behind me tapped my shoulder
I turned around to look over
She pointed to the floor and said
"You dropped your money"
Is this another four-leaf clover?
First, I said, "it can't be"
Then I said, "no it must be"
Finally, I said "thank you"

I came from the shop and outside
Looked inside my pockets and realised
The 5 euro on the floor really wasn't mine
I couldn't believe my eyes
Now I have two
This was confirmation, not just a sign
I just knew
It felt too good to not be true...

The secret to living is giving

Wizard

I like the word super
I like the word natural
I love what isn't factual

or deemed to be, seem to be
seem to see...see, it seems
seen, the unseen it seems
shifting paradigms in these times
we share a lot in these times
see the unscreened in these times
hear the unheard, in these rhymes

Cold and late night in January,
I feel an erosion to past commotions
Blocks of own scolding
Blocks of own coding
If a belief is a thought you keep thinking
I'm generally recoding

Wanting to be
Rich Spiritually
Coming to be
Enriched Spiritually
Is it all the years I put in?
The taste of discovery
The clock froze, when I touched it
No cloak, for this prose, as I touch it

A flashback, to lights on 1st January
The colours shined right above me
As they danced and flickered in delight
I felt fire, heart warm desire
12:00 am on 1st January
When the sky shines for a few minutes
I filmed this experience
This could be typical but I felt gifted

Held thoughts of appreciation
Counting my blessings as I expressed
My love and gratitude for this life
The fireworks had finished, I went inside
Before I closed the door, hear
a noise from outside
A firework from the sky landed on the floor
Found its way to my garden
As I picked it up, I looked up in the sky's distance
A final firework exploded right
above me, in bright liberation
This one fell right at my feet whilst I witnessed
I read on the paper attached to
it - it said 'Sky Wizard'
Looked back up to the sky's message

Write it and it is determined
In Christmas, wrote I'm like Merlin
Wizz Air took me somewhere
I owe it to my spiritual path
Following earnest

The next letter is hidden
Thick feathers hidden
A silent flight on a silent night
Messages
Coming to be given

Onward

Onward
Seen magical workings in my poems
Now, where did these come from?
This is literal, this is physical
I didn't expect this
When asking to hear a call
I saw a reflection of my spiritual work
A mirror call

Before
Uncanny coincidences
Synchronistic moments
Angelic guidance
What then....
When, things happen beyond our imagination?
We question...
Was it really just our questions?
Is this my doing or beyond my happening?
We live on a mysterious planet with pure magic

you see, you and me
we're like...alike
you see. you; me
We're the kind to sought for
thoughts, there is more...
We kinda, sorta, thought...there is more

Followed guidance from the highest
I took the flight here
I entered the shop, on the wall it said, Grace
I guess I'm in the right place
Felt the shopkeeper knew me
Felt he knew something - beyond everything
By the look on his face...
With the few words, he chose to say

Prayed in my poems, God pave me a way
There is only so much he will pave
I really did come to make
decisions along the way...
I do have control and more of a say...
Thank you for all you showed
to me up till this day

Technically

Let's talk about sci-fi
Movies are becoming like real life
Life really is a movie, that's
more what it's really like
The World's becoming connected
with Mobiles and WI-FI
Maybe one day, there will be more
intelligence than human intelligence
It's called A.I
It could constantly improve its own
intelligence at the same time
They say a fool makes the same mistake twice
Though we have no miss-takes
in this movie we call life
Just lessons as blessings

Technically - technology is supposed to free us
Though some say it's the most enslaved times
Deluding us from terror
Equally, times of most awakenings
Alluding to an illuminating era
A.I will eliminate the human error
Did you hear the human era?
Forever they will repeat of
eliminating human terror
What part of their game, are you not aware of?

Dare I, say I worry
In our inevitable turning
Life's movie screen
Literally moving to screens
The larger part of you exists in technology
Though it is a small reflection of you
It's like the extension of you
We exist in screens, in everything that moves

Yet we are empowered by this technology!
What will we do?
What will we bring?

Family you chose

Heard your family is whom you chose
That is before coming here too
It is a belief, that very few hold true

Sometimes I think, my father made some money
To show me, money isn't everything
From early I questioned the material
A kid out there hustles for income
Because his Dad thought money
wasn't everything
I don't see a disconnection, I see the contrast
What if you chose them, to give
you unique situations?
For you to find what you want
For you to find who you are
So you seek forward
Ingredients in this pot
I see what is
And I'm grateful for what I've got

Sometimes, I think my mother is who she is
To show me, what blessings love can bring
To be open-minded enough
For me to share her my mysteries
Over many years,
Feels good to be transparent

On how I want to see through
Parents do and don't, understand you

My parents always thought...
A job is something for me to do
Over the years, I had to become myself
I built my character, over these years
Standing firm in my curiosity
Admiration for love and for truth

Sometimes I think, my older brother is in my life
For me to learn how different I am
How we all are
Stand proud in your uniqueness
Since, time to time, I may victimise myself
For wanting to share my light
Negativity on my mind and life
He's always been a reminder, to be myself
To never dampen my shine
Sometimes we want to be so alike
To get things right

I can't get darker and light you up
I can't get sicker and make you feel better
I can't get drunk, help you to sober
I can't be asleep and wake you up
It's true and neither can you

Family can be a reminder of
what is unconditional love

Family members, can guide you or thwart you
Just look above
Giving us endless opportunities
To grow from love

Sometimes, I think I chose my younger brother
So, I'll be an older sibling, to find advice in myself
Naturally
Since, he allows me to gleam
Wants me to beam
The light that is in me

I heard your family is who you chose
They help you to develop through
Indirectly too
Directly - it's up to you

When you see differences as truth
When you use, the love that is in you
When you notice, what God has chosen for you

Bring you joy

Bring in your joy we need it,

Keep it so natural

It's seamless,
So, may seem less

Still, bring your joy
Somebody will feel it
It'll ease stress

Love is pure
Unnoticeable
When we feel stress

Bring in your joy
Never needless,
Never need less

Bring in your joy we need it

God's projection

We are all God's children
Feel it in my Spirit
Hear it with no Godly inflections
See signs as Godly reflections
God plays mysterious testing
For our introspection

If we are part of God's creation
Then, we are God's intention
Then, we are God's projection
As we create, in touch with source
We are God's expression
Keeping up with our expansion

As I journey here...
My mind likes to find what is wrong
What could be wrong, is available all the time...
So is what is good - it is always there
What is good - is the love in me
I can it pull the good from anywhere
When we receive the feeling of connection
Then we're feeling God's affection
God is everywhere
If we're worried
We have God's protection
When we're feeling torn with a decision

God's surgery has accuracy
When you're torn with his incision

Layers to you
Layers to God
Many layers
Mainly just one
Love

Architect

I talk to God a lot
In my mind, it's not this guy at the top
It's not this guy
Though, I may refer to God as him in rhymes
I see a book on a higher shelf
I see the Bible, I've sung hymns and rhymes
I see religious books, like the Quran with it
Though, I haven't fully read the
Bible or raised by the Quran
I know beautiful things exist
in between their lines

We all have in us innocence
We feel it - in a sense
Felt by our inner sense

What's art that's direct?
It's hard to detect
Every artist pours their heart out,
Till their heart will rest
Till your heart & their heart connects
This heart won't rest and wants tests

Let's capture, all the art to take
Seeing with your eyes
Seeing through a phone
There's an architect, behind the art in tech
As so, there is wordsmith behind the word spins

Let's capture, all the art awake
Seeing with your mind
Seeing through your soul
There's an architect, behind the heart and breath

Thoughts of appreciation turn to
Thoughts of inspiration to
Feelings of expansion and more
Knowing of connection and the maker of all

Looking outside the box
I'm like David Blane, fasting on television
I'm manufacturing my hunger for something
Since I've always had food for thought
Now I'm bulimic to the conditioning
I'm starving for wisdom and my
stomach is rumbling

There are no rules
Plus, no perfection, besides nature
What's a God, that gave you
everything you want?
Here you go, that is all, there you are
Where is the fun?
What else is there, if you got it all done?

So thoughtful, watching inspired thoughts form
As I go through another portal
Immortal cords on
Uni-verse means one song
This life is your song

Kobe Bryant

Kobe Bryant, the name sounds familiar
Is he a basketball player?
His name has travelled somewhere over here
I watch football, I don't have an idea
Yet, I've seen his videos and it's very clear
He has a mentality that I could adhere to

He called it mamba mentality
Not bowing down to mediocrity
Smell your dreams...it's potency
We all have potent dreams
Let's dive deep, into this potent sea
What can we free by going in deep?
What can we find by rising to the tides?
Like a slam dunk and jumping head high
When you over-deliver, it's a sight
Like three-pointer while being pushed backward
When you score and not go down without a fight
When you decide, in whatever you do
You don't just try
You want to be the greatest of all time
There was a reason why a light
shined from above
Down on the ground on Kobe's crash site
As if God said, come home...
I'm proud - it's time

Legends

Legends live their truth and never die
A mystery why some legends
die so soon in this life
If there are two truths, is there a lie?
If it sounds too good to be true, is it a lie?
If there is one truth, is it available all the time?
Our legends come in many forms
We are all legends in our lives, only some realise

Take away my real lies
I know have real eyes to realise
It's there in front of me, to go forward
It's here inside of me, to go inward
It's there outside, for me to go outward
It's here in front of me, to go onward

They say Legends can change the hands of time
Some say Legends, can rearrange
the plans of time
Their crane of determination
Lifting the unwritten book of our future
Adding a lovely spin to the story
Once they've ascended

Late October

Late October...
Found a missed call from a fairy
I dial back, what will it tell...
A fairy tale?
Maybe...
It's amazing
I have a friend who's turning to what life be
I got an old friend
She's like..." like"; yikes
She really likes likes
She might, might till the end of her life
Pretend to be Kylie
While figuratively... Kylie's
pretending to be Queen B
It's so beautiful when they act from the inside
It's where their queen be
That's where their beauty lies
Just how some women carry themselves
It's for your eyes
That's just me, that just what I see

This insight inspired
Is ignited by a song from Russ
I hear as I write this
The song is called 'Celebrity'

Winter is approaching
Crystallise thoughts like snow
While autumn is here
I will shed my dead leaves
Getting to the root of a poet's tree
As I write this poetry

Artist of my life
Writer of my story
Back to the drawing board
I'm drawing swords for markers
Finding myself as an artist
Never drawn, to draw when I am bored
It's always been more...always was told...
Imitation is the highest form of flattening
Don't come short
To what is rising naturally

Ruminating

I'm much of a philosopher
Meditative like Rumi waiting
There is always room I'm making
For ruminating...

Till 3 pm, school was in tuition
But 24/7, school is intuition

If you're silent- listen
Listen in silence

If words take you somewhere silent
You're never far from home
Your soul will be your asylum

I took less on, I took the lesson
Trust, because I'm protected

All these dreams
Let them grow like a swelling
Let them go like a swelling
Let go of the dwelling

Flick back a decade, all in a split-second
A decade, for it to all come in a split-second

Three Messages

Love is all

Love exists in animals, to show us, love is beyond just humans. Nature exists, to show us, life, beyond animals. Stars exist to show us, more life, beyond nature here. The Sun touches us all, shows, we are supported by life - beyond earth.

Is life - support?

They all co-exist, connect and support each other, which is the same nature as us. Since we bring more to life; through our support. Then, are we from beyond the earth too...?

Support sounds, contextual. Read it again and change support to love.

Travel alone

In a book, that just has a chapter, that really
to you, makes no sense in relation to what is
going on, you try to understand it, then you
rather play with it, let go of the exact narration
to what it will be and how it all plays out.
Except you know the heading of your mental
travel log is - 'Every day is an adventure'.
Once, travel alone and see for yourself.
Finding it an 'experience' is beside the point.
Whatever it will be...it will be your experience.

Reading in-between, the lines

On my way to the train station, I bought myself a book from a bookshop near it, right before heading in. Whilst inside the station, I quickly made my way to catch a train, but first I had to go buy myself a ticket for my journey. Whilst I waited and held my new book in my hands, so keen I was eager to read it in the queue before purchasing my ticket. I was very tempted to read in-between the lines but I chose to wait, till I got on the train and seated.

At some point, whilst I was waiting in the queue, a lady said something very inspiring to me after we striked up a conversation, something I was thinking about earlier. Then right after, whilst I was about to get on the train, the man in front of me, kindly gestured for me to go in front of him, out of nowhere. Giving me a greater opportunity to find a better place.

I hopped on the train and as I was walked to find a suitable seat, I smiled & thought to myself, "I'm glad I didn't read in-between the lines, otherwise those interactions may have never occurred".

Once, I located my seat and got seated, before finally opening my new book. I saw on the cover in small writing, 'This book is a reminder, that good things do happen'. I paused and smiled again, because I read in-between the lines.

Printed in Great Britain
by Amazon